DIY Christmas Paper Quilling Greeting Card

DEDICATION

Contents

Quilled Christmas Tree Card

Ingredients

- Paper quilling strips
- Green colored craft paper
- Slotted quilling tool
- Pencil
- Scissors
- Glue

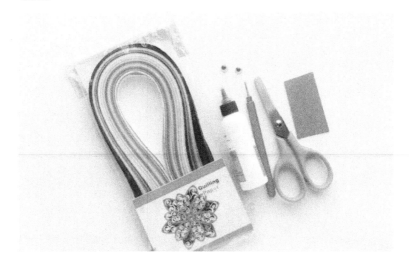

Christmas Paper Quilling Greeting Card

Instructions

1. Select 3 different shades of green colored quilling strips for this craft. I'm using 6 inches long strips and 12 inches long strips to create the different quilled shapes for this craft.

2. Take a strip and coil it with the help of the slotted quilling tool. Carefully take out the coiled strip from the tool and allow it loosen up freely.

3. Press the loose coil on any point to form a teardrop shape. Glue the open end to secure the shape.

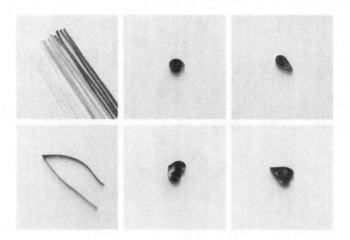

4. Take a 12 inches long strip and fold it into half.

5. Coil the 2 open ends of the folded strip. Coil all the way to the closed end (near the half fold part). This will form a heart shape.

6. Take the teardrop shape formed in step 3 and place it inside the heart shape (between the 2 twirls of the quilled heart shape).

7. Take a 6 inches long strip and coil the whole strip from any one

end to form a twirl shape. Take a same colored quilled teardrop shape and attach it with the quilled twirl on its straight side. Create teardrops, heart shaped pieces with a teardrop inside and teardrop with a twirl attached to it.

8. Grab more paper quilling strips and create more quilled shapes.

9. Cut out a piece of green colored craft paper and grab all the quilled shapes.

10. Let's start from the top part of the tree. Grab 3 small teardrop shapes and attach them on the top side of the craft paper by keeping the pointy ends of the shapes facing upwards.

11. Continue to attach the quilled shapes downward by keeping a tree shape in mind. For the next layer below the first quilled layer, I've attached a heart shape with a teardrop attached in the middle, teardrop with twirls attached on both sides and on the 2 outer sides, I've attached 2 teardrops.

12.　　Grab different shaded quilled shapes for the third layer. Simply glue the quilled shapes downwards but forming a wider layer than the previous layer.

13.　　For the fourth layer I used the darkest colored quilled shapes. You can add more layers if you want to. If you are confused about the pattern, you can place the different quilled shapes on the paper before gluing them.

14.　　Cut out the craft paper around the quilled patterns outer border. Quill a 5 point star pattern using yellow colored quilling strips and attach it on the top end of the quilled tree.

15.   Quill 4 loose coils using brown colored quilling strips and attach them on the bottom side of the quilled tree by forming a square shape with the 4 brown loose coils. Also, create some tight coils from red and other bright colored strips. Attach the tight coils between the quilled shapes of the tree randomly to decorate the Christmas tree.

Quilled Christmas Lights Card

- Heavyweight card stock
- Quilling paper strips
- Slotted quilling tool
- Craft glue
- Scissors

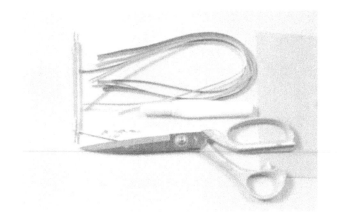

Take a 20 inches long colored quilling strip and use the slotted quilling tool to coil the entire strip. Once the coiling is done, take out the coiled strip from the tool and allow it loosen up.

Press any one side of the loose coil to form a teardrop shape and glue the open end to secure the shape.

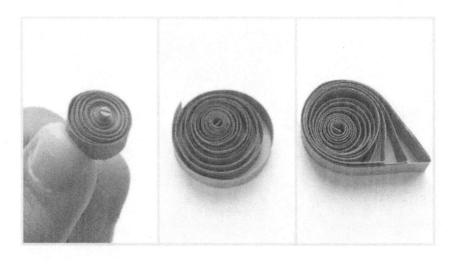

Take a 3 inches long white colored quilling strip and create a loose coil shape with it. Press 2 opposite sides of the loose coil to form a lens shape.

Take the teardrop shape prepared in the previous steps. Insert the lens shape created in step 5 into the teardrop shape, through the gap of any coils near the curved end – this forms a bulb.

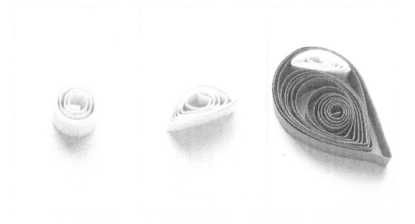

Use the above process to create as many different colored Christmas light bulbs as you like.

Use a 6 inch long black quilling strip and create a small twirl on any of its ends. Use about 2 or 3 cm to create the twirl pattern. Repeat with a second black quilling strip.

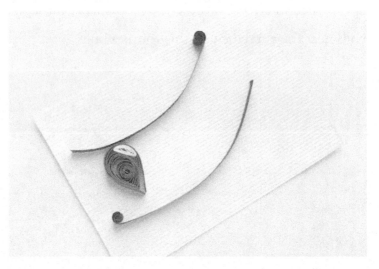

Glue the 2 black twirled strips on the paper by creating a slight curvy pattern with them. Glue the 2 strips in 2 rows, keeping at least an inch gap between them.

Glue your brightly colored paper Christmas light bulbs and glue them along the black "wire," keeping the curved ends of the bulbs adjacent to the black strips.

Allow the glue to dry and write your own unique Christmas message on the front of your card.

Gilded Tree Card Ornament Tutorial

Card Making Supplies:

- Card stock - red, green, metallic gold
- Paper trimmer with cutting and scoring blades (or use a bone folder to score card stock)
- Double-sided tape or glue stick - to adhere card layers
- Ribbon - plaid, about 3/8 inch x 5.5 inches
- Hole punch - for tree lights, 1/8 inch

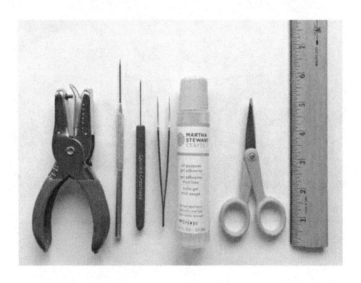

Christmas Paper Quilling Greeting Card

Quilling Tools

Quilling Supplies:

- Quilling paper - 1/8 inch standard width; gold-edge ivory, red
- Paper piercing tool - to apply glue to quilled coils (or use a pin, toothpick or your quilling tool)
- Quilling tool
- Tweezers - fine-tip
- Glue - I like to use clear gel adhesive
- Scissors - detail
- Ruler
- Plastic lid or waxed paper - to use as a glue palette and work board
- Damp cloth - to keep fingers and tools free of glue

Card Making Steps:

1. Cut a piece of red card stock that measures 4.5 x 10.75 inches. Score and fold at the 5.125-inch mark to create an uneven side-fold card that measures 4.5 x 5.5 inches when closed. This allows room for the ribbon to show along the right hand side when the card is closed.

2. Referring the the photo, draw a 5.5-inch tree on green card stock and cut it out. Score and fold the left edge under 1/4-inch and use double-sided tape or a glue stick to adhere the fold around the card spine.

3. Punch gold metallic ornament dots/stars and glue them in place with the help of tweezers.

4. Use tape or a glue stick to adhere the ribbon along the right side of the card.

Quilled Ornament Steps:

Christmas Paper Quilling Greeting Card

If you are new to quilling, learn the basics in post.

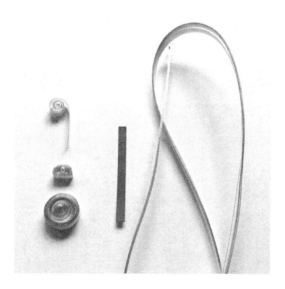

1. Roll a loose coil using a 13-inch strip of metallic-edge ivory quilling paper. When the strip has been rolled, slipped off the tool and allowed to expand, pull the end to create a thickened outer edge to define the shape. Glue the end.

2. Butt a 2-inch strip of red quilling paper against the end of the ivory strip and glue it once around the coil.

3. Make a rectangle using a 5-inch strip of metallic-edge ivory quilling

paper. To make a rectangle, first make a marquise shape by pinching opposite sides of a loose (round) coil, then turn it slightly and make another set of opposite pinches. Glue the end at a corner and trim any excess paper.

4. Make a loose scroll as the ornament hanger using a 3-inch strip of metallic-edge ivory quilling paper.

5. Glue the three quilled components together on a non-stick work board and adhere the ornament to the tree.

Christmas Paper Quilling Greeting Card

Quilling Tips:

- Brand new to quilling? Take your time and practice until your fingers become used to working with narrow strips. It's only paper and glue... you can do this!

- Use the smallest amount of glue possible for a neat look.

- Tweezers are helpful when gluing quilling to a card. For example, use them to gently touch the underside of the ornament to a shallow puddle of glue that you have spread on a plastic lid or waxed paper, and place it directly onto the card. Don't slide it around as that will leave a shiny snail trail of glue.

Paper Quilling Stocking Card

Materials and tools needed in making this quilling paper stocking Christmas card:

- 5mm Red Quilling Paper
- 5mm Yellow Quilling Paper
- 5mm Green Quilling Paper
- Plastic Paillette Star
- Model
- Rolling Pen
- Scissors
- Tweezers
- Glue

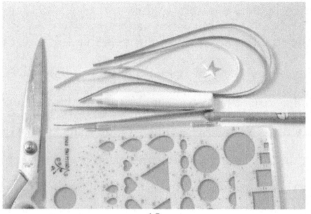

Christmas Paper Quilling Greeting Card

Instruction on making the quilling paper Christmas tree with stocking:

Step 1 : Shape a stocking with quilling paper beads

1st, cut enough pieces of 5mm quilling papers (about 5cm long), then roll them with a rolling pen one by one;

2nd, modify them into 8mm beads;

3rd, stick the quilling paper to the card one by one to form a sock image as shown.

Step 2: Add white quilling paper beads

1st, cut enough pieces of 5mm quilling paper (about 5cm long), and roll them into 8mm beads one by one;

2nd, stick the white quilling paper beads on the top of the sock and shape it as pictured.

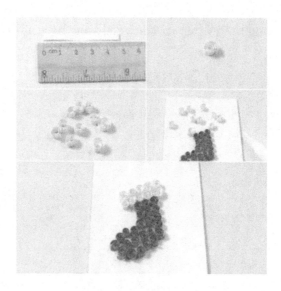

Step 3: Finish the quilling paper stocking card

1st, cut a piece of 5mm green quilling paper, and stick the 2 ends together;

2nd, stick the green sling to the proper position of the quilling paper sock;

3rd, Add other ornament as you like on the card.

Finished the paper quilling christmas card with stocking in 15 minutes. The basic procedure is to roll the paper beads and then shape the stocking.

Make Paper Quilling Candles Cards

Materials and tools in making the new year quilling paper card:

- 5mm Red Quilling Paper
- 5mm Yellow Quilling Paper
- Card
- Quilling Models
- Scissors
- Quilling Pen
- Glue
- Tweezers

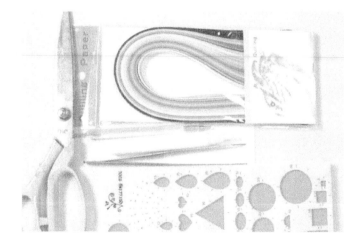

Christmas Paper Quilling Greeting Card

Instructions on making the quilling paper new year card:

Make red and green petals

1st, cut 5 pieces of 5mm green quilling papers, and 5 pieces of 5mm red quilling papers(each about 19.5cm long);

2nd, roll the quilling papers with a rolling pen and put them to 12cm size hole to adjust one by one;

3rd, stick the tail, hold and fix one point with tweezers and press the other end with fingers to make it a petal-like shape as pictured;

4th, repeat this process to make the rest petals.

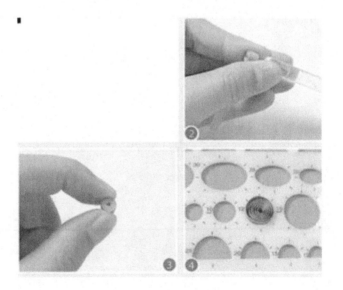

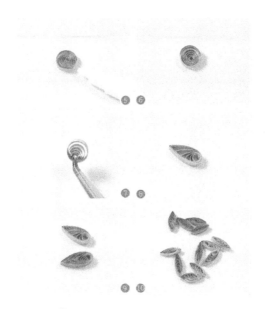

Make quilling paper flowers

1st, prepare a piece of card paper, stick 5 green petals on bottom part of the card;

2nd, stick the rest 5 red petals on the surface of the green flower as pictured;

3rd, cut a small piece of 5mm yellow quilling paper, and roll it into a small bead;

4th, stick the yellow quilling paper bead to the flower to make it a bud.

e

Step 3: Add additional ornaments

1st, roll another 2 pieces of red quilling paper (about 25cm), and make them into snail shape as shown;

2nd, stick the ornaments in opposite positions and trim them.

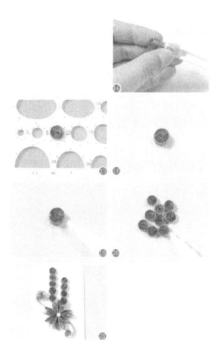

Step 4: Add quilling paper candles

1st, cut 9 pieces of red quilling paper (about 10cm), and roll them into 8cm beads one by one;

2nd, stick 5 red quilling paper beads to the left side and the other 4 beads to the right side as pictured;

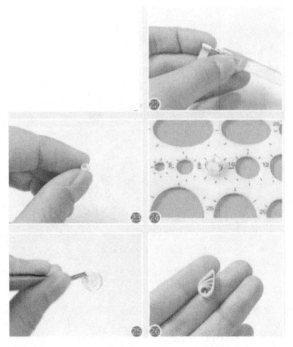

3rd, cut 2 pieces of yellow quilling paper and roll them into 8cm bead respectively;

4th, fix one end with tweezers and press the other end to shape them;

5th, stick them to the top of the candles respectively.

Christmas Paper Quilling Greeting Card

Time for the final look of this quilling paper card!

This quilling paper greeting card is finished

Paper Quilling Christmas Bell Cards

Supplies in making this paper quilling Christmas bell card:

- 5MM Yellow Quilling Paper
- 5MM Bright Red Quilling Paper
- 5MM Green Quilling Paper
- 5MM Black Quilling Paper
- 6MM Yellow Ribbon
- White quilling card
- White Glue
- Rolling Pen
- Scissor
- Glue Gun
- Glue Stick

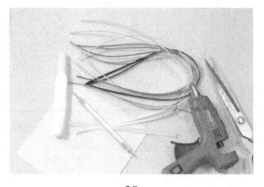

Christmas Paper Quilling Greeting Card

Step 1 : Roll a pattern of the Christmas bell

1st, roll a circle with bright red quilling paper, disperse it a lot and stick the end;

2nd, pinch it to oval, like an eye, pinch crease of the outer 2 layer, and stick several layers at the same point.

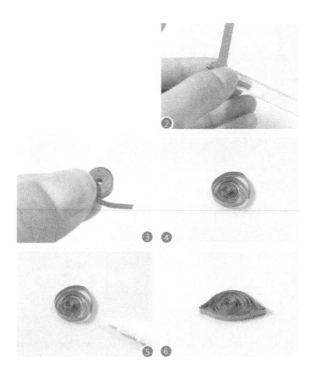

Step 2: Make a Christmas bell base

Make a shape of bell with black quilling paper, inset the pattern into the bottom of this shape, and stick it firmly.

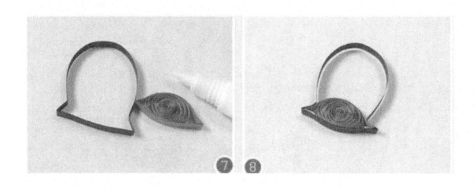

Step 3: Make 2 Christmas bells

1st, roll a circle with yellow quilling paper, later pinch the outer several layers to a quadrilateral;

2nd, make other 2 quadrilaterals, inset them to the bell base;

3rd, roll an incompact circle with bright red quilling paper, just stick it to the top part of bell base;

4th, roll 2 small circles with bright red quilling paper, stick them to the top of quadrilateral;

5th, roll a small circle with yellow quilling paper, stick it to the bottom of Christmas bell. Repeat all the steps and make another one.

Step 4: Make 3 leaves

1st, roll a circle with green quilling paper, after several layers, pinch paper to a rhombus and around several circles, stick the end firmly; 2nd, repeat above step and make other 2 leaves.

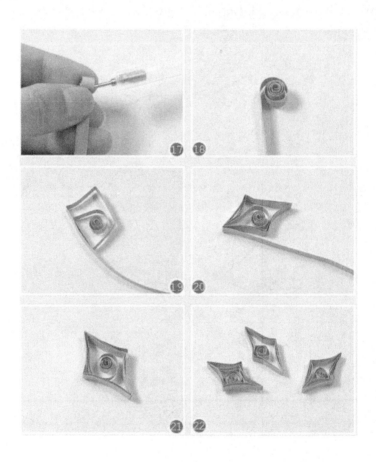

Christmas Paper Quilling Greeting Card

Step 5: Stick all the patterns together

1st, stick 3 green leaves with 2 Christmas bells firmly, glue them on the white quilling card;

2nd, make a bowknot with yellow ribbon, stick it to the Christmas bell, just like the picture below.

Here is the final look of the paper quilling Christmas bell card.

With quilling papers at hands, you can make this quilling Christmas bell card, it's so colorful and lively, right? This quilling Christmas bell card have many different shapes, you can also pinch it to other shapes, just you like

Card Combination Snowflakes and Christmas Trees

Supplies needed in DIY the easy Christmas cards:

- 380x3mm Green Quilling Paper Strips

- 380x3mm Quilling Paper Strips

- Card

- Scissors

- Iron tweezers

- White glue

- Rolling pen

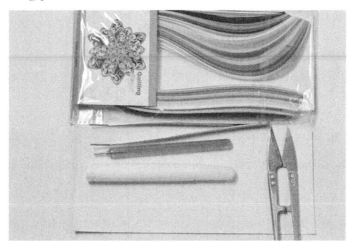

Christmas Paper Quilling Greeting Card

Step 1: Make the Christmas tree

1st, fold the heavy green quilling paper as the Christmas tree shape;

2nd, continue to make the "Christmas tree";

3rd, make another Christmas tree with light green quilling paper, please see the picture below.

Step 2: Paste the "Christmas tree"

Paste the "Christmas tree" on the 2 sides of the card with white glue.

Step 3: Roll the ribbons

1st, roll two pieces of red quilling paper as ribbons with the rolling pen;

2nd, paste the ready red ribbons near the Christmas tree, showing as the picture below.

Step 4: Roll the yellow charms

1st, roll two pieces of yellow quilling paper as the pen shape with the rolling pen;

2nd, paste the "pen" under the Christmas tree, showing as the picture.

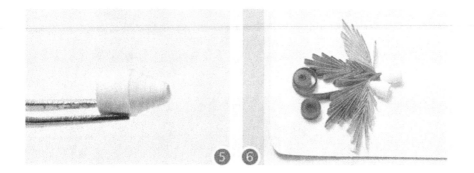

Step 5: Make the snowflakes

1st, roll 3 pieces of white quilling paper like the picture below shows;

2nd, roll the white quilling paper as the snowflake shape.

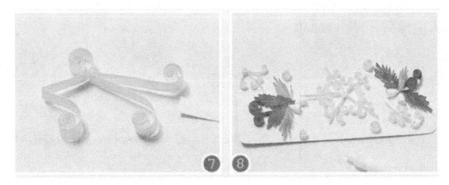

Step 6: Finish the Christmas card

Paste the "snowflakes" on the card, showing as the picture below.

Here is the final look of the easy DIY Christmas card.

Snowflakes Paper Quilling Christmas Cards

How to make the paper quilling shapes

Diamond

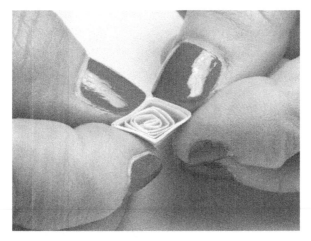

Press the coil flat between your thumb and forefinger, release the coil. Then reposition your thumb and forefinger over the pointed ends, and press flat again. Open the diamond shape out.

Teardrop

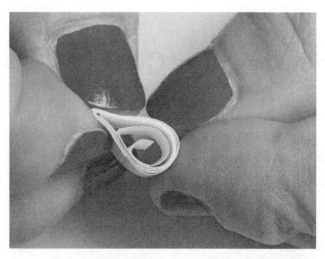

Pinch the coil at one end, using your thumb and forefinger, to create a point.

Eye

Pinch the coil at both ends using your thumbs and forefingers.

Square

Make an eye shape, then pinch the other two sides to form a square.

Tight heart

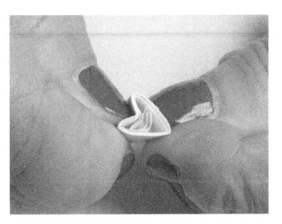

Make a teardrop then put a dent in the rounded end using your thumbnail.

Loose heart

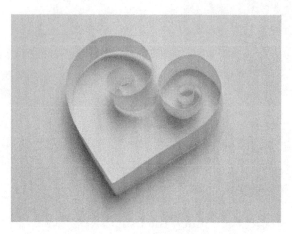

Fold a strip in half, twist one end round a cocktail stick then roll loosely by hand until you have created one half of a heart. Repeat this step on the other end, rolling the strip in the opposite direction.

For all three paper quilling cards, you will need

- Strips of paper
- Cocktail stick
- PVA glue

How to make a mint green snowflake paper quilling card

We used 5mm-wide strips and a 15 x 10.5cm grey card blank

Christmas Paper Quilling Greeting Card

You will need

Large snowflake:

- 12 x 30cm mint green strips

Medium snowflake:

- 6 x 30cm mint green strips
- 6 x 20cm grey strips

Tiny snowflake

- 6 x 15cm mint green strips

Christmas Paper Quilling Greeting Card

Instructions

1. Roll six tight coils from mint paper, glue and set to one side. Roll six loose coils, glue then pinch them to make diamonds.

2. Apply a little glue to the edges of the six diamonds and stick them together to form the snowflake. Glue six tight coils in between each diamond.

3. Repeat to make the medium snowflake, using grey paper to make the tight coils.

4. Finally make the tiny snowflake and glue all three snowflakes to the front of the card.

Top tip: Using a pair of tweezers can help when picking up your coils and gluing them in place.

How to make a white snowflake paper quilling card

We used 1cm-wide strips, a 10.5cm square lilac card blank and a 8cm square piece of mint green paper.

Christmas Paper Quilling Greeting Card

You will need

- 14 x 30cm white strips

Instructions

1. Roll five tight coils, glue and set to one side. Roll five loose coils, glue then pinch them to make eye shapes.

2. Glue all five eye shapes together to form the snowflake. Then glue the five tight coils in between each eye shape.

3. Roll a further four loose coils and pinch to make them into teardrops.

4. Glue the snowflake to the centre of the mint green paper and a teardrop in each corner. Then glue to the front of the lilac card front.

Christmas Paper Quilling Greeting Card

How to make a blue, white and grey snowflake paper quilling card
We used a combination of 1cm-wide and 5mm-wide strips, a 15cm square pale blue card blank and a 10cm square piece of metallic blue paper.

You will need

- 6 x 30cm white strips (1cm-wide)
- 6 x 20cm blue strips (5mm)
- 1 x 10cm blue strip (5mm)
- 6 x 20cm grey strips (5mm)

Christmas Paper Quilling Greeting Card

Instructions

1. Roll three tight grey coils, and three tight blue coils, glue and set to one side. Roll six loose white coils, glue then pinch into teardrops.

2. Roll the shorter strip of blue paper into a tight coil, glue, then stick the white teardrops around the edge. Then glue alternating grey and blue coils in between the six teardrops.

3. Make three loose grey hearts and three loose blue hearts. Glue the coils of the hearts to the snowflake, so the points of the hearts face out.

4. Stick the snowflake centrally on the blue metallic paper, then stick to the card front.

Made in the USA
Las Vegas, NV
06 May 2024

89578901R00031